YO-CCC-362

YOU MUST REMEMBER THIS

1952

MILESTONES, MEMORIES,
TRIVIA AND FACTS, NEWS EVENTS,
PROMINENT PERSONALITIES &
SPORTS HIGHLIGHTS OF THE YEAR

TO :
_____

FROM :
_____

MESSAGE :
_____

_____

selected and researched
by
mary a. pradt

WARNER ⓦ TREASURES ™

PUBLISHED BY WARNER BOOKS

A TIME WARNER COMPANY

COPYRIGHT ©1995
by Mary A. Pradt
All Rights Reserved.

Warner Books, Inc.
1271 Avenue of the Americas
New York, New York 10020

Warner Treasures is a
trademark of Warner Books, Inc.

Ⓦ A Time Warner Company

DESIGN:
CAROL BOKUNIEWICZ DESIGN
PRINTED IN SINGAPORE
FIRST PRINTING : MAY 1995
10 9 8 7 6 5 4 3 2 1
ISBN : 0-446-91028-7

'52

Strikes and labor disturbances continued to disrupt the economy. In March a series of tornados swooped down like dive-bombers in five Mississippi Valley states, leaving 200 people dead and over 2,500 injured. Entire towns were wiped out in Missouri, Tennessee, Arkansas, Alabama, and Mississippi.

Dwight David Eisenhower, Supreme Allied Commander in Europe and World War II hero, revealed in January that he was willing to run for the Republican presidential nomination. At the July GOP convention in Chicago, Ike was nominated on the first ballot. His running mate was Richard M. Nixon, 39,

newsreel

a California senator who had gained national attention in the House Un-American Activities Committee's investigations of alleged Communist Alger Hiss. A reluctant Illinois Governor Adlai Stevenson was the Democratic nominee. In September, Senator Nixon gave his famous "Checkers" speech on national TV, defending his $18,000 slush fund, his wife's "respectable Republican cloth coat," and the little cocker spaniel dog that daughter Tricia named Checkers. Nixon declared, "I am not a quitter." Ike promised, "I will go to Korea." The Ike and Dick team was elected by a landslide in November, with a record voter turnout.

In one political upset, **john f. kennedy,** 35, won a Democratic Senate seat, beating Republican heavyweight Henry Cabot Lodge in Massachusetts.

The Allies launched major air strikes against North Korea in May, hitting several cities hard with napalm, machine guns, and bombs.

international

headlines

King George VI died in February, and **Princess Elizabeth,** 25, rushed back from holiday in Kenya to assume the throne. Elizabeth's son Prince Charles Philip Arthur George, only three years old, became the British heir apparent.

IN FRENCH INDOCHINA, THE FRENCH FORCES GOT DRAWN FURTHER AND FURTHER INTO THE GUERILLA WAR BEING WAGED BY THE VIET MINH. IN OCTOBER, THE FRENCH TROOPS LAUNCHED AN OFFENSIVE AGAINST HANOI AND GENERAL GIAP'S COMMUNIST FORCES.

In Egypt, in July, a military coup forced King Farouk out; the Egyptian king was known as an international playboy.

In Jordan in August, Crown Prince Hussein, not quite 17, was named by Parliament to succeed his unstable father, King Talial. The father had been mentally ill and under treatment in Swiss clinics for years.

5

a tall, blond g.i. named george

flew to Copenhagen, underwent 2,000 hormone injections and six surgeries, and flew back to New York as Christine Jorgenson, 26, the first transsexual to go public.

GENERAL MOTORS ANNOUNCED IN JULY THAT IT WOULD OFFER OPTIONAL AIR-CONDITIONING ON SEVERAL OF ITS FORTHCOMING MODEL CARS.

JACKIE ROBINSON January 9 became the highest-paid player in Brooklyn Dodger history.

cultural
milestones

SAMUEL BECKETT'S *WAITING FOR GODOT*, A PURPOSEFULLY INTERMINABLE TRAGICOMEDY ABOUT TWO HOBOS WAITING FOR A RESCUER, PREMIERED.

for at-home entertaining,

"the year's most exciting new idea for modern living" was the Servel "Electric Wonderbar," a portable, silent "refrigerette styled as smart furniture." Cold drinks, snacks, and ice—two big trays of ice cubes—could be right at your elbow. It could even be wheeled out to the porch or patio and ran on regular current.

television

By 1952, more than one third of American homes had TV (34.2%). There were 15.3 million TV households.

A Congressional subcommittee investigated ethics in TV. Committee members June 3 outlined TV's moral faults. They deplored the proliferation of violence on TV crime shows and the omnipresent beer and wine ads.

top-rated shows of the 1952 fall season:

1. "I Love Lucy" (CBS)

2. "Arthur Godfrey's Talent Scouts" (CBS)

3. "Arthur Godfrey and His Friends" (CBS)

4. "Dragnet" (NBC)

5. "Texaco Star Theater" (NBC)

6. "The Buick Circus Hour" (NBC)

7. "The Colgate Comedy Hour" (NBC)

8. "Gangbusters" (NBC)

9. "You Bet Your Life" (NBC)

10. "Fireside Theater" (NBC)

On TV in 1952, Allen Funt hosted the TV version of his radio show "Candid Microphone."

No-Smear Lipstick

CANDID CAMERA

brainpower or bisquick?

A survey showed that college women lagged far behind the rest of their sex in 1952 in the matter of getting married. Only 69 out of 100 college women were married at the time of the survey, compared with 87 percent of all U.S. women.

On TV, weekdays at 10:30 A.M. on CBS-TV, "Bride and Groom" aired and kept an estimated audience of more than two million housewives enraptured. In its sixth year on radio, then TV, "B & G" had received over seventy thousand applicants wanting to be married off on the air. The producers chose such worthy grooms as a Douglas Aircraft exec, a Phi Beta Kappa, an atomic scientist, 17 policemen, and a Medal of Honor winner. The newlyweds

milestones

received a weeklong vacation, with everything except liquor paid for by the show, and the loan of a Pontiac. Sponsors showered the couples with gifts from vacuum cleaners to silverware. The ceremonies themselves ran about four minutes, and only rabbis and Protestant ministers presided, because Catholic ceremonies were required to be in a church or a rectory. The brides ranged from age 17 to 75, the grooms from 19 to 78.

'52

DEATHS

Eva Perón,
charismatic wife of Argentina's president, Juan Perón, succumbed to ovarian cancer July 26, at the age of 33. "Evita" was a heroine to the *descamisados*, the "shirtless ones," but she also was ruthless.

Harold Ickes,
FDR's Interior Secretary, died February 3.

Maria Montessori,
Italy's first woman physician and founder of the Montessori Method of educating children, died in the Netherlands May 6, at the age of 81.

John Dewey,
the famous educator and philosopher who revolutionized school systems in Chicago and New York, succumbed to pneumonia June 1. He was 92.

Chaim Weizmann,
First Israeli president, 77, considered the Father of His Country and a great humanitarian, died November 9, after a long illness.

Charles Maurras,
French writer known for his Royalist politics and role in the Vichy regime, died November 16 at 84. He had been convicted of wartime treason but got out of a life sentence because of illness.

births

ISABELLA ROSSELLINI, born June 18, one of the beautiful twin daughters of Roberto Rossellini and Ingrid Bergman, has had a film career since the mid-seventies, and since her divorce from Martin Scorsese. She also, in 1982, launched a highly successful modeling career, gaining an exclusive, lucrative contract with Lancome cosmetics.

JEFF GOLDBLUM, actor, was born October 22.

CHRISTOPHER REEVE, actor, was born September 25.

MARILU HENNER, actress, was born in Chicago April 6.

PIERCE BROSNAN, actor, was born in County Meath, Ireland, May 16.

SUSAN DEY, actress, was born in Pekin, IL, December 10.

GRACE JONES, model/singer/actress, was born in Spanishtown, Jamaica, May 19.

DAVID BYRNE, musician, was born May 14.

TOM PETTY, rock star, was born October 20.

CATHY RIGBY, gymnast, was born in Long Beach, CA, December 12.

JAMES SCOTT CONNORS, U.S. tennis star, was born September 2.

BILL WALTON, pro basketball star, 1978 MVP, was born November 5.

11

'52

hit music

1. **blue tango**
   leroy anderson
2. **wheel of fortune**
   kay starr
3. **cry**
   johnnie ray
4. **you belong to me**
   jo stafford
5. **auf wiedersehen, sweetheart**
   vera lynn
6. **i went to your wedding**
   patti page
7. **half as much**
   rosemary clooney
8. **wish you were here**
   eddie fisher
9. **here in my heart**
   al martino
10. **delicado**
    percy faith

1. **with a song in my heart**
   jane froman
2. **an american in paris**
   soundtrack
3. **south pacific**
   original cast
4. **singin' in the rain**
   soundtrack
5. **i'll see you in my dreams**
   soundtrack
6. **show boat**
   soundtrack
7. **the king and i**
   original cast
8. **the merry widow**
   soundtrack
9. **johnnie ray**
   johnnie ray
10. **because you're mine**
    mario lanza

Patti Page

Eddie Fisher

top R&B singles

1. **lawdy miss clawdy**
   lloyd price
2. **have mercy, baby**
   dominoes
3. **5–10–15 hours**
   ruth brown
4. **goin' home**
   fats domino
5. **night train**
   jimmy forrest
6. **my song**
   johnny ace
7. **one mint julep**
   clovers
8. **ting a ling**
   clovers
9. **three o'clock blues**
   b. b. king
10. **juke**
    little walter

JOHNNIE RAY, KING PLEASURE, EDNA MCGRIFF, SONNY THOMPSON, ROSCOE GORDON, AND SUNNY GALE ALSO APPEARED ON THE R&B CHARTS.

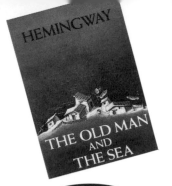

HEMINGWAY

THE OLD MAN AND THE SEA

fiction

1. **the silver chalice**
   thomas b. costain

2. **the caine mutiny**
   herman wouk

3. **east of eden**
   john steinbeck

4. **my cousin rachel**
   daphne du maurier

5. **steamboat gothic**
   frances parkinson keyes

6. **giant**
   edna ferber

7. **the old man and the sea**
   ernest hemingway

8. **the crown of glory**
   agnes sly turnbull

9. **the saracen blade**
   frank yerby

10. **the houses in between**
    howard spring

bestselling

books

the new york yankees

completed a four-year sweep in the American League and defeated the Brooklyn Dodgers in the World Series.

THE DETROIT RED WINGS WON THE WORLD PRO CHAMPIONSHIP WITH AN EIGHT-GAME SWEEP IN THE STANLEY CUP TOURNAMENT.

SPORTS WERE SUFFERING FINANCIALLY IN 1952; BASEBALL AND BOXING SHOWED DECLINING GATE RECEIPTS. BASKETBALL STILL REELED FROM THE PREVIOUS YEAR'S BRIBE SCANDALS. THE NCAA LIMITED FOOTBALL GAMES ON TV TO ONE BIG GAME A WEEK.

sports

rocky marciano was the first heavyweight champ since Joe Louis beat Jim Braddock in 1937.

OLYMPICS

Interest in sports ran high, with the added attraction of the 15th Olympic Games, held in Helsinki. The biggest star to emerge was phenomenal distance runner Emil Zatopek of Czechoslovakia, who always looked as if he were in pain. His wife, Dana Ingrova Zatopek, beat the previous Olympic record with her javelin throws. After a twelve-year absence, the Soviet Union was represented, but they lost to the Americans, 553.5 points to the U.S.'s 614. California-born two-time decathlon champ Bob Mathias announced he would rest on his laurels and retire at age 21.

HORSE RACING

Alfred G. Vanderbilt's Native Dancer and Mrs. Walter Jefford's One Count were horses of the year. Attendance at the U.S.'s running tracks was up 12 percent in 1952, totaling about 27.5 million.

'52

box-office champs

1. **The Greatest Show on Earth** ($12 million)
2. **Quo Vadis** ($10.5 million)
3. **Ivanhoe** ($7 million)
4. **The Snows of Kilimanjaro** ($6.5 million)
5. **Sailor Beware** ($4.3 million)
6. **The African Queen** ($4 million)
7. **Jumping Jacks** ($4 million)
8. **High Noon** ($3.4 million)
9. **Son of Paleface** ($3.4 million)
10. **Singin' in the Rain** ($3.3 million)

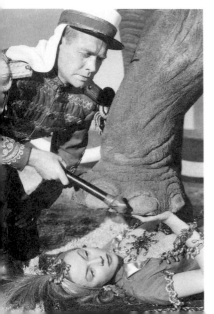

Winner of the 1952 Academy Award Best Picture was **The Greatest Show on Earth.** Other nominees were High Noon, Ivanhoe, Moulin Rouge, and The Quiet Man. **John Ford** won Best Director honors for **The Quiet Man,** beating Cecil B. DeMille, John Huston, Joseph L. Mankiewicz, and Fred Zinnemann. **Gary Cooper** won Best Actor honors for **High Noon,** over Marlon Brando in Viva Zapata!, Kirk Douglas, Jose Ferrer, and Alec Guinness. Best Actress was **Shirley Booth** in **Come Back, Little Sheba.** She beat Joan Crawford, Bette Davis, Julie Harris, and Susan Hayward. **Anthony Quinn** took Supporting Actor honors for his role in **Viva Zapata!** over Richard Burton, Arthur Hunnicut, Victor McLaglen, and Jack Palance. **Gloria Grahame** in **The Bad and the Beautiful** took Best Supporting Actress honors, over Jean Hagen, Collette Merchand, Terry Moore, and Thelma Ritter. Writing awards went to **The Greatest Show on Earth, The Bad and the Beautiful,** and **The Lavender Hill Mob.**

1. Dean Martin
& Jerry Lewis

2. Gary Cooper

3. John Wayne

4. Bing Crosby

5. Bob Hope

6. James Stewart

7. Doris Day

8. Gregory Peck

9. Susan Hayward

10. Randolph Scott

movies

the first feature-length 3-d movie

WAS RELEASED: *BWANA DEVIL*. VIEWERS GOT POLARIZED GLASSES TO CREATE THE ILLUSION.

THIS IS WHEN CINERAMA PREMIERED. THIS WAS A BREATHTAKING TECHNICAL PROCESS THAT MADE THE VIEWER FEEL SURROUNDED—A THREE-DIMENSIONAL FEELING WITHOUT THE NEED FOR GLASSES. MANY CINERAMA SEQUELS, BASICALLY FANCY TRAVELOGUES, FOLLOWED.

Interest in foreign-built sports cars caused Packard and Buick to develop sporty models, although they were not yet in production. The Packard Pan-American had wire racing wheels, a rear-mounted spare, and an 185-hp engine. The Buick Skylark also had chrome-plated racing wheels and such sug-

'52 cars

The trend to V-8 engines continued

gestions of sports car styling as swept-down doors and cutaway fenders. One sweet convert was the Mercury Monterey 1953 model that debuted in fall 1952.

horsepower supremacy

CONTINUED TO BE CONTESTED. FUEL ECONOMY WAS IMPROVING. THE YEAR SAW POWER STEERING AND POWER BRAKING COME INTO MORE WIDESPREAD USE. AN INNOVATION THAT APPEARED WAS THE AUTOMATIC HEADLIGHT DIMMER.

AIR CONDITIONING
WAS OFFERED FOR THE FIRST TIME AS AN OPTION.

Peck *and* Peck

Wherever you see Braemar you're seeing Scotland's finest

Come spring, and *naturally* you'll bloom in Braemar's newest. A short-sleeved cardigan with ribbed trim up the button front, bordering the flattering mandarin neckline. White, light blue, Scottish rose. 34 to 40 . . . 29.95.

BRAEMAR

RK • CHICAGO • BOSTON • PHILADELPHIA • BALTIMORE • DETROIT • CLEVELAND • ST. LOUIS • MINNEAPOLIS • ST. PAUL
APOLIS • ATLANTA • WASHINGTON, D.C. • CINCINNATI • KANSAS CITY • MILWAUKEE • HARTFORD • BUFFALO • PROVIDENCE
1956

HATS BECAME HIGHER, POINTIER OR SLOPED TO ONE SIDE. ELABORATELY JEWELED EVENING CAPS WERE A NICE FORMAL LOOK.

fashion

fashion trends

COLOR WAS THE BIG STORY, AS FASHION DESIGNERS TRIED TO LURE WOMEN AWAY FROM THEIR GRAY FLANNEL SUITS, NAVY SHAUNTING DRESSES, AND CAMEL-COLORED COATS. PURPLES, GOLDS, GREENS, BLUES, AND REDS FILLED THE FALL STORE WINDOWS. PARIS'S FALL COLLECTIONS, HOWEVER, SHOWED THE RETURN OF THE LITTLE BLACK DRESS.

The **"miracle fabrics"** of synthetic yarns got more attention. The **"sweater girl"** look came back into popularity. The **"poodle cut"** and ponytail were the favorite of younger women, though some went glamorous with soft waves and **"Mamie bangs,"** imitating the incoming First Lady's neat forehead ringlets.

FUR STOLES HIT THEIR PEAK OF POPULARITY IN 1952.

MACHINE-WASHED LAST NIGHT

Sounds incredible, doesn't it? Yet it's an amazing fact: you can machine-wash these lovely sweaters! Just use a warm-water setting. Let your Acrilan sweater tumble or drip-dry. Not ship it on. What do you see? A sweater that hasn't shrunk, hasn't stretched, hasn't changed a whit. It's as shape-perfect as ever . . . yet you didn't waste a minute blocking or measuring. If you're as busy as you are smart . . . if you hate dishes that need out-fitting . . . you'll love sweaters of luxurious, machine-washable Acrilan acrylic fiber.

for men, a single-breasted suit,
white shirt, and tie were the fashion basics, although sportswear was a little more fun. A real man, of course, owns a few snappy hats, such as Dobb's Hankachif Felt number at $10, or Dobb's "lightweight town hat," with the Air Foam Guild Edge, for $20.

final factoid

**mr. & mrs. potato head
were available for $1.98**

25

archive photos: inside front cover, pages 1, 5, 8, 11, 15, 21, inside back cover.

associated press: pages 2, 7, 16.

photofest: pages 4, 6, 9, 10, 12, 13, 18, 19.

original photography:
beth phillips: pages 14, 22, 23, 25.

album cover:
courtesy of bob george/
the archive of contemporary music: page 14

photo research:
alice albert

coordination:
rustyn birch

design:
carol bokuniewicz design
mutsumi hyuga

'52